Can I Come Down Now Dad?
Five Sugars Please
Those Were Your Father's

Sam and Barry (pocket size CD cassette)

Available in Aladdin

John Hegley

Love Cuts

with drawings by the author

Mandarin

If you have any comments or suggestions to pass on
or would like to be on the author's
(very occasional) mailing list,
write to:
Hegleypost, Methuen Publicity Department
Michelin House, 81 Fulham Road, London sw3 6rb

A Mandarin Paperback
LOVE CUTS

First published in Great Britain 1995
by Methuen London
This edition published 1996
by Mandarin Paperbacks
an imprint of Reed International Books Ltd
Michelin House, 81 Fulham Road, London sw3 6rb
and Auckland, Melbourne, Singapore and Toronto

A CIP catalogue record for this book
is available from the British Library
ISBN 0 7493 2194 6

Printed and bound in Great Britain
by BPC Paperbacks Ltd
a member of The British Printing Company Ltd

Contents

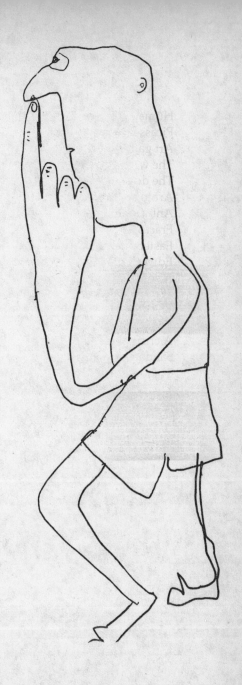

My first love

He was a grey-blue glove puppet dog
which I called Pete
which I sometimes gave some of my dinner to
and which he didn't eat.
He couldn't bark
but he always got the top mark
in my cloth-eared classroom.
He had only one beady eye
and on the other side was a vacant wire
but still my desire
for Pete
was complete.
It was not a problem that Pete did not eat
his dinner
because love does not need
to force-feed
a puppet
even if it does need to put its hand up it.

3

Good afternoon

One of the things a poet does is to put
usual things in an unusual way
so instead of saying good afternoon
the poet may wish you
a boonful second spoonful of the day.

A lover of words

The words are his potatoes.
He spades them out
he lets them lie
he brings them home
he wrings them dry.
Then the honing
and the boning
of the artificial eye.
And then further cleaning:
this is Seamus,
Heaning.

The genie that never materialised

When I was a teeny boy
I used to enjoy
my father's stories about a certain genie of his own
    imagining.
Mind you, I seem to remember him moving the
    action along
by asking me questions about what was going on:
'And what do you think the genie did next, John?'
Like the lessons at school which involved fooling you
into thinking that you were having fun.
But one day in the middle of a certain genie
    adventure
there was a seeping of weeping from my dad
and he said he never had
the happiness of making a genie story
because his dad left him when he was only a boy;
as if he was there to talk about the woe in his own
    life
rather than bring the singing into mine.

After the alien landing

Itchy dog.
Toffee's filthy car-rug infestation
was so bad
that he had
to have a muzzle
to stop him nuzzling
and guzzling himself with his fore-teeth.

There was one section of his back
with a population so dense
that it needed shaving
so that it gave the impression
of a square corn circle
in a field of fur.
The peeled scratch patch.
The revealed pink pitch of no flea's land.
Toffee's problem.

Skip

My dad escorted me to the hut
the day I went along to join the cub scouts
and after I had joined in some of the games
Skip took us to one side, asked us both our names,
then asked me if I was enjoying myself
and when I said that I was
he told me that being a cub scout
was about having fun but
it was also about duty, decency and paying your
    subscriptions.

And I looked at my dad because
he was listening like a little boy;
looking back I think
Skip was like the father my father never had,
the protector, the advisor
and the authority above,

my dad was like a little lad with the gift of love.
He was in the grip
of Skip
and when we got home he stated
that we had been in the presence of a great man
and I felt sad
that the parent is only expected to attend on the
      recruit's first visit
and I said 'I bet you wish you could go again
      yourself Dad'
and my dad said that I had a cheek
and that he would be going along every week.

Down in Witches' Dell

Absconded from primary school
and another day of swirling torment
beside my childhood dream girl;
in the pond within the wood
a stick stood
strangely upright.
I dreamed it was Excalibur,
waded in and fished it out
splashed back to the bank
made out our initials
on the blank bark,
then waving the wand about
I wished a bond between us
a fondness that wouldn't fade
a sticking together for tomorrow
and for ever
in the spreading future
beyond the deadly nightshade.
Meanwhile in the playground she was snogging
        someone else.

My father shows his teeth

One morning my dad asked me to comb my hair
before leaving home for school
and I said no
then quickly picked up my blazer
and exited the bungalow.
Half way up the road
I heard running feet behind me;
I turned to find my father
chasing me with the comb
and a very red face.
I sped off, sure that his older frame
would lose in a race
but his pace was made faster
by his need to show me who the master was
and at the top of the street
he stopped me, stretching and grasping my collar
and spinning me hard against the wall.
For a while we stood together gasping,
quietly he offered me the comb, telling me
that if I didn't tidy my hair
he'd come down the school
and do it for me in front of all my friends.
I didn't actually have any friends
but thought it best to smarten myself up anyway.

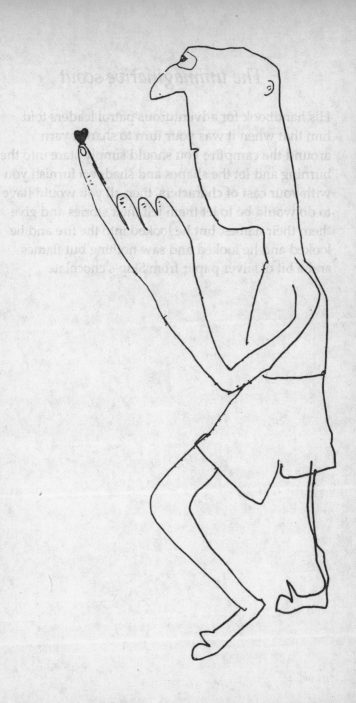

The unimaginative scout

His handbook for adventurous patrol leaders told
him that when it was your turn to share a yarn
around the campfire you should simply stare into the
burning and let the shapes and shadows furnish you
with your cast of characters, then all you would have
to do would be to let them tell their stories and give
them their names, but he looked into the fire and he
looked and he looked and saw nothing but flames
and a bit of silver paper from Skip's chocolate.

Autumn verses

Autumn is strange stuff
anagram of Aunt mu
but not of nostalgia.

Scarves come out, clocks go back
faulty or otherwise,
pumpkins enjoy brief popularity.

Kids collecting cash
for slouched-on-the-ground
ash-bound bad dressers.

Ore tummy, heart of mould
old leaves leaving
enter the cold.

Last October
I got very depressed
when our dog got knoctober.

Luton Library verses

It was opened by the monarch
and it meant a lot to me
in my early years in Luton Town
beside the river Lea.
Four new books a fortnight
I'd turn up to lend
and as I turned the pages
each one turned into a friend.
In time I was a shelving lad
so I could spend all day
a-walking round the library
a-working for no pay
but I wasn't discontented,
please don't read me wrong:
they'd given me a shelvers' badge
and somewhere to belong.
And the first poem I ever wrote
went in the magazine
of the Library in Luton
which was opened by the Queen.

Luton versus Middlesbrough

Five whole goals to Luton Town
and Middlesbrough not one,
but though their team was five-nil down
their fans were up for fun
and when their consolation came
before the whistle blew
they echoed Luton's 'we want six'
with a modest 'we want two'.

Holy day of observation

On a curve of pavement
I observe the fourth person in a row
to pass me with a grubby forehead.
In a flash I remember Ash Wednesday,
the ritual church besmirchment
with smudgy crosses.
At the bus stop
a smoker drops a matchstick,
I pick it up
and ministering unto myself
with the blackened remains,
in front of my brains
I make a sacred thumbprint of my own.

The halo and the dozy dozen

The Lord was born without sin
but not without his thin flat halo.
The wise men they were reverent,
the shepherds they were coarser:
'That shiny, floating hat,' said one
'it's like a flying saucer.'

In his last years
the Lord would regularly cast his halo
into the wilderness
as part of his dog's exercise regime
and he once tried to amuse his disciples
by holding it like a steering wheel.
'What is it, boys, a bus or a car?'
'But we don't know what buses or cars are, Lord'
answered his bewildered team
and the Lord set his dog unto them.

Jazz poem

Jubilant
Argumentative
Zig
Zag

Journey
Around
Zapadabba
Zoo

Juju
Alto
Zooming
Zimmer frame

Jazz clubs they are open
when folk are in their beds
jazz is not a sleepy word
though half of it is zeds

The old lady loves

Grandma loves her daughters
and grandma loves to dance
grandma will dance anywhere
if given half the chance
but the chances come in quarters.

Sore

I'm sore
I've got love no more
I'm sore
I'm a hinge with no door
and no screws.

A perk on the way to work

Against the flow
of returning revellers
the unaccustomed early bird
puts out his hand to slow
the racing red.

Full moon in the near side mirror
he hears the concertina door
deliver a sliver of tune
as it offers admittance.

Seeing the colour of his money
the driver offers him advice
'It looks very nice
but there's a conductor.'
Giving thanks he enters the sanctum of the saloon
in need of a nap and reassured
that there's somebody on board
with whom to discuss his dreams.
He's always preferred teamwork
to the one-person-operated system.
No bus is an island.

The emergensea

The octopus awoke one morning and wondered what
    rhyme it was.
Looking at his alarm-clocktopus
he saw that it had stopped
and it was time to stop having a rest
and get himself dressed.
On every octofoot
he put
an octosocktopus
but in his hurry, one foot got put
not into an octosock
but into an electric plug socket
and the octopus got a nasty electric shocktopus
and had to call the octodoctopus
who couldn't get in
to give any help or medicine
because the door was loctopus.
The octopus couldn't move, being in a state of
    octoshocktopus
so the octodoctopus bashed the door
to the floor
and the cure was as simple as could be:
a nice refreshing cup of seawater.

Swimming channels

To satisfy the preference for
tailor-made programming
there will eventually be
so much telly on TV
that it will work out at one channel per person
which won't help with convers'n'
about the shared experience
of what was on the box last night.

Sandman

The sandman
slips through his own fingers
the sandman's home
is his sandcastle
the sandman times his eggs to perfection
the sandman is an island
the sandman
avoids beach holidays.

Pancake man

He's Shrove Tuesday's number one fan.
All those minds
simultaneously mixed up in the flour and batter
making the matter more powerful:
he believes that a
shared experience is greater than
the sum of its ingredients.
The world is his frying pan
and he is a bit of a tosser.

Yule do

```
                    W
                    H
                    E
                    N
                   TH
                  E CH
                 RISTMAS
                TREE WAS
               BOUGHT DAD
              DIDN'T GIVE IT
             MUCH THOUGHT;
           HIS SON WANTED A
          VERY STRAIGHT TOP TO
         SUPPORT HIS BLUE PETER
       SILVER PAPER STAR, DAD JUST
     WANTED SOMETHING REASONABLY
   CHRISTMAS TREE SHAPED THAT DIDN'T
                    D
                    O
                ANY DAMAGE
                TO THE PAINT
                  WORK OF
                  THE CAR.
```

George

At fourteen I was enamoured with a girl in another class and an opportunity to make her aware of my feelings was provided by the annual third-year discothèque. I hadn't been to one before being as you were only in the third year once and it was an annual event, but knowing that she was going meant that my attendance was compulsory even though I was an isolated boy detested by many.

I asked my dad what he thought I should wear and he immediately advised my school uniform. 'You haven't got any other clothing,' he reasoned. Arriving at the function I felt like a fool, seeing everybody else in their casual cool but I was brightened by the sight of the one who drove me to drool. There was also a boy in the room whom I yearned for but kids in those days were such fascists where sexual politics were concerned, and I spurned my unfashionable feeling, revealing only my yearning for the girl. Our twirl together was a predictably poor piece of choreography and I'm sure that she was only doing it because I promised that if she did one dance with me I would never bother her again.

I was shortly to find a different input for my love and output for my passion in the shape of Luton

Town Football Club and our dream of promotion from the Fourth Division. My involvement with the team also provided my first successful amorous encounter – with the boy I'd been frightened to approach in the discothèque. It was on the coach back from the away match at Hartlepool. Away from home and also away from the aggressive rigidity of the other boys we chatted and batted our eyelashes and coming back I nestled deep into his soft mum-made jumper and dropped into a sleep. When the coach stopped I got up, sad to be back, but happy to have experienced such happiness, only to discover that we were only at the motorway services near Derby and there was still a load more snuggling to be had with the lad and I glowed on the road, inwardly root'n' and toot'n', going back to my abode in Luton oblivious to the uselessness of our centre-forward's shoot'n'.

Omo

We were fourteen
and the two of us went camping
and you smuggled into my tent
and we snuggled
and in the morning your smile was a joy
but when we were back at the school
because I was a boy
and so were you
we had to keep it under the covers
otherwise the others
would have taken out their fears on us
but it was our fear as well
and back at the school
even when there was no one else near
all we ever spoke about was football.

Autograph hunters

There were about half a dozen of us,
we were thirteen or so
and we used to go down to the match
and stay behind to catch
the players on their way out
after having caught them once already
on the way in.
But after two or three seasons
the other boys started coming to the game
for the joys of the game only;
it seemed they had all outgrown
the amassing of autographs
and being as harassing the players alone
had no appeal for me
I too left my collecting books at home.
And how I missed that name-scribbling scurry,
it was the saucer of the FA Cup
but more than that, unlike my companions
I wasn't in a hurry
to grow up.

History was hers

She wanted to convey
how an olden day
was formerly the topmost peak
of life so far so to speak:
'time's furthest outpost,
the very tip of time,' she would say.
She wanted us to feel how
'once upon a time' was once as real as now.
She wanted to make the distant past
and its cast
as vivid as playtime.
History was there to be enjoyed
and she would be very annoyed
if someone wasn't listening
and she would be livid
if you were seemingly daydreaming,
and lost in another world.

Self-pitying poem

Poor
Old
Egocentric
Me.

Humanist poem

Part
Of
Everyone,
Me.

Picasso poem

Pablo
Oblong's
Educated
Mess.

Art gallery address

For three reasons I'm pleased
to have been summoned
to come and
open this exhibition.
Firstly because I feel
these creations will appeal
to your average punter
even though they have ambiguity,
in a world where everything must have a box to go to
here is a lack of meaning
without a lack of merit.
The second reason is the fact
of this being a public foundation;
as such it is part of the shared,
the commonly held
and I believe that the more
people have in common, the more
they have as individuals.
And the third reason
is the money.
But it's a long long way behind the other two.

The wrong oblong

This man walks up to the Tate's controversial bricks
and picks one deliberately from the pile.
The bricks are unblocked,
I am quite shocked
the nearby attendant is too
and appearing unsure of what to do
she orders the bloke
to put back the breakaway brick
and smiling a cocky sort of smile
he returns the piece,
but not to its original place.
As he paces away
the attendant chases him
saying that he should put it where it was
and the man says he won't because
he feels he has made an artistic improvement.

The dog smoggler

I sit in the gallery beside a man who is stroking an imaginary dog. An attendant comes over and asks him to remove the creature from the premises.

'But it's only a pretend dog,' I protest on the muttering man's behalf.

'I'm sorry,' replies the official, 'but the only pretend animals of any description which the gallery permits are confined to the exhibits.'

Then the man announces that his dog has had an accident.

'What kind of an accident?' barks the attendant.

Art to enjoy

In the gallery I found
the pictures did not touch me,
they were just patterned patches
spread around the wall
which is maybe all
they were meant to be.
Spread upon the ground
was some artifical turf
which was good inside a gallery
but still I didn't get the pictures
so it wasn't good enough.
I remembered the same stuff
was once laid down
on the earth at Kenilworth Road
where I supported Luton Town
and I thought that as a popular spectacle
this art exhibition was not a patch
on the potential for passion in a football match
and I could sympathise with those who'd say ditch
the public subsidy
and knock it off the price
of paying to get in to see
the artists on the pitch.

Anti-Cantona poem

Push
Off
Eric.
Merci.

Fracas

Eric got aerobic
when the going got too Francophobic:
he didn't have a leg to stand on
but he had someone to land on.

'FOUL'

Easter offerings

In Liverpool I witnessed *The Murder*
whilst walking round the Walker Art Gallery.
I've heard talk that Cézanne
was a man too busy applying his eye to the apple
to grapple
with life's grimmer realities,
but here I found the grimness to be great;
even the murderer's trousers seemed to radiate
an essence of murderousness.
The splayed victim and the descending knife
conjured a depiction
of the pinning down for the Crucifixion
and made me realise the loss of that life
for the murder that it was;
mind you, can it really be said
to be murder
if the victim picked himself up and rose
from the dead?
Like those nails through his hands
this was a man
who was truly driven.
Come back Jesus
all is forgiven.

In Luton I told my tiny four-year-old sister
that the outer shiny paper
was more valuable than the inner chocolate egg
and she agreed to swap her egg for my paper.
And then, needy for chocolate
she offered her paper for my egg
and I said I'd been pulling her leg
but she was welcome to beg.
For a segment.

Edward the First

One day Miss brought in a big box of books and said that we could choose one each to take home but she wanted us to do the choosing in an orderly fashion. 'Right, I want those at the front to come out and choose first,' she said, and all of us in the front row got up and to everyone's surprise Eddie got up as well, even though he was in the second row. And Miss said, 'Where are you going Edward?' and Edward explained that it is the same as when you talk about the front of a desk: there is the very narrow bit beyond the groove where you put your pencils which is the exact front, but for practical purposes, because there are no words for the bits in between, the front actually extends right back as far as the middle.

A somewhat absent-minded attempt to be politically correct

Someone I don't know that well
tells me they have a little boy.
'Oh yes,' I enquire, 'and how old is he or she?'

The quest for
the holy spectacles

JOHN (sings).

> It's lies about the wise men
> because there was one more
> and like the other wise men
> a Christmas gift that wise man bore.
> He bore the sacred spectacles
> to help the Saviour see,
> and not just in the manger
> but in his job in Galilee.

HARRY.   Here you are lads, here's your teas.

JOHN.   Thanks Harry, and two vegetarian breakfasts when you're ready.

HARRY.   And what's your mate having?

TONY.   I'll have the same if it's all the same with you.

HARRY.   No problem.

TONY.   What's that book about, John?

JOHN.   It says that the Lord wore glasses.

TONY.   I didn't know they had glasses in them days – but I suppose if you can raise yourself from the dead, you can get yourself a pair of glasses before they've been invented.

JOHN.   That's right Tone, and he left them behind in
the tomb because you don't need glasses in
heaven.

TONY.   Did anybody fetch them out?

JOHN.   His dog did. And buried them straight after.

TONY.   I didn't know he had a dog. Was it called
Fishy?

JOHN.   Yes.

HARRY.   Here you are lads, vegetarian breakfasts
twice, twice.

TONY.   That was quick.

HARRY.   Cheers. They don't call me Hurry for
nothing. In fact, they don't call me Hurry at all.

JOHN.   Some believe the glasses found their way
into the hands and onto the head of Harold.

TONY.   Harold who?

JOHN.   Harold who was in Hastings.

HARRY.   Do you want a sweet as well lads?

TONY.   What have you got?

HARRY.   Toffees or liquorice sweets.

JOHN.   Can I have a liquorice sweet?

TONY.   I'll have a toffee, thanks.

JOHN.   Yes it seems that Harold wore them in the
battle; in fact, they were the cause of it. William
wanted to get hold of the glasses because he
believed they could make him immortal, or
improve his eyesight at least.

TONY.   They didn't do Harold much good.

JOHN.   Unfortunately he'd just taken them off to clean them when the arrow hit him. Apparently William saw Harold's death as a bad omen and threw them into the sea.

TONY.   An appropriate end.

JOHN.   If it was the end.

HARRY.   Here you go lads, one toffee, one liquorice sweet.

JOHN.   Harry, you're a man of some experience, what do you think happened to the holy glasses?

HARRY.   I'd put my money on Glastonbury.

TONY.   Why's that then?

HARRY.   Until the thirteenth century it was known as Holy Glassestonbury.

TONY.   It wasn't was it?

HARRY.   No. I tell you what though, instead of all this talking . . .

TONY.   Well this is Glastonbury but where do we start to look?

JOHN.   Remember, when the pupil is ready the teacher appears.

TONY.   So where's the teacher?

HARRY.   How about this woman with the dog?
           Hello love, you haven't seen the holy glasses
           have you?
MRS SISTER.   Is that a pop group?
HARRY.   Sorry. I was talking to the dog actually.
MRS SISTER.   No you weren't.
HARRY.   Just a little joke.
MRS SISTER.   I enjoyed it.
HARRY.   What's his name then, is it Fishy?
MRS SISTER.   Yes it is.
HARRY.   Hello Fishy, you haven't seen the holy
           glasses have you?
FISHY.   Ruf, ruf, rrrrroooof.
MRS SISTER.   He says there were a couple of corn
           circles in the shape of a pair of glasses a few
           years back.
TONY.   Incredible.
FISHY.   Rough, ruf ruf.
MRS SISTER.   He says what's more incredible is that
           it was a field of potatoes before they appeared.
TONY.   Really?
FISHY.   Ruff ruff ruff ruff ruff ruff ruff ruf. Ruff ruff
           ruff ruff ruf.
MRS SISTER.   No.
FISHY.   Ruff ruff ruff ruff ruff ruff.
HARRY.   What's he saying now?
MRS SISTER.   It's drivel I'm afraid, French drivel

44

actually. You might try looking in that direction. I'll give you a ring if he comes up with anything else. *Au revoir.*

TONY. *A bientôt.*

MRS SISTER. Come on Fishy. Don't do that Fishy. Fishy!

JOHN. Hold on. Come back!

TONY. They've gone John.

HARRY. What's glasses in French?

JOHN. *Lunettes.*

TONY. Or *verres.*

JOHN. Versailles. Of course.

HARRY. Let's give it a go shall we? . . . .

JOHN (*sings and swings*).

We seek the holy glasses
We travel near and far
We seek the holy glasses
and now we're going Eurostar . . .

TONY. Do you mind if I open these shutters Harry, I love the drifting sound of a foreign street.

HARRY. How come we have to go round town asking people if they know anything about the holy glasses while John just sits in the library?

TONY. It's all part of the same job isn't it?

HARRY. Yes but when you consult a French book about the holy glasses it doesn't look at you as if you're stupid like a French person does. And how come John automatically gets the double bed?

JOHN. Hi boys. Any luck?

HARRY. I luckily avoided a couple of punches down by the railway station.

JOHN. Well I've made some real discoveries. You know the Alouette song?

TONY (*sings*). *Alouette, gentille alouette, alouette je te plumerai, alouette* – shall we do it as a round?

JOHN. No. Apparently that song was composed in William the Conqueror's time.

HARRY. I don't see the link.

JOHN. It actually used to go '*Les lunettes, la-la la, lunettes, les lunettes, je les porterai*'.

TONY. He brought the glasses back from the battle of Hastings after all then?

JOHN. Yes, he thought he'd be safer trying them on on home ground; in case Harold had put a vibe on them. He had himself crowned with them in church on the site of what is now Rouen Cathedral.

HARRY *and* TONY. Yeah?

JOHN. Yeah. But when he got off the throne he walked straight into a pillar.

TONY.   And then had them thrown into the sea?

JOHN.   Yes, I'm afraid so.

HARRY.   So now we're going to go fishing for them are we? I've had enough of this.

JOHN.   Hold on Harry, there's a few other leads I wanted to follow up in the library while you continue to walk around asking the French people for clues and getting a load of abuse . . . What's up with him? Why did he just up and go like that?

TONY.   He needs something a bit special in his life and he thought he was going to find it with us, but all he's gone and done is lost a lot of trade at the caff.

JOHN.   It's a sacred quest though, Tony. You can't expect it to be over in five minutes: it's not like looking for a pair of glasses down the side of the settee.

TONY.   Well, Harry's been gone three days now and my feet hurt and there's no sign of the object of our search.

JOHN.   But we could get an old pair of secondhand specs, do them up, take them back to Harry and tell him they're the real thing and bring some sparkle back into his eyes.

TONY.   A customised crown of glasses? . . .

Bang bang . . . saw saw . . . nail nail.

TONY.   They're coming on really nice.

JOHN.   I like those stained-glass lenses.

TONY.   Thanks John, what are you making, wooden
side-pieces?

JOHN.   Yes, the French for side-pieces is *les branches*.

TONY.   Like 'branches'.

JOHN.   Yes they are a bit aren't they. Harry's going
to be so surprised.

TONY.   And we'll do them for him at cost price?

JOHN.   Plus labour of course. Now what we need to
do is to make him believe he can see something
special.

TONY.   I don't get you.

JOHN.   With the stained glass everything's going to
look really blurry . . .

TONY.   . . . And we help him along with the
interpretation of that blurriness . . .

JOHN.   *Absolument* . . .

JOHN.   Hiya Harry we're back. Four teas please.

HARRY.   *Bonjour* boys. Welcome home. Sorry I went
           a bit morose out there, it's just that there's a
           general emptiness in my inner life.

JOHN.   Well we've got some good news.

HARRY.   About the general emptiness in my inner
           life?

TONY.   Unfortunately no.

JOHN.   But we've found the holy glasses.

HARRY.   Where were they?

TONY.   Down the back of the settee. Here they are.

HARRY.   Fantastic.

JOHN.   Try them on then.

HARRY.   Are you sure I'll be all right?

JOHN.   Are they safe spex you mean? Well you'd
           best take precautions: keep your hands cupped
           under your face in case they fall.

TONY.   It looks a bit like someone praying.

JOHN.   Probably the origin of the gesture.

HARRY.   It all looks a bit blurry.

JOHN.   You're experiencing two places at once.
           You're here with me and Tony but you're
           somewhere else as well.

HARRY.   Eh?!

JOHN.   Look Harry look! Look at the people looking
           at you for a sign that you are the Messiah.

TONY.   There's five thousand of them Harry.

JOHN.   And they all want their dinner.

HARRY. It's all a bit blurry, I'm afraid.

JOHN. Don't be frightened Harry.

TONY. Trust in the glasses.

HARRY. No . . . it's not happening.

BURRY (*mobile phone*). Bur bur.

JOHN. Hold on Harry, I'll just take this call.

BURRY. Bur bur.

TONY. Your phone's ringing John.

JOHN. I know it is, that's why I said I'm just going
to take the call . . . Mrs Sister! Hello. Any news
on the holy glasses?

HARRY. I thought these were them.

TONY. I'm afraid we've deceived you somewhat.

HARRY. You've made me bear false glasses.

MRS SISTER. I just wanted to tell you that the dog's
just done a huge lake of wee and started barking
with a Scottish accent.

JOHN. Glasses-go?

MRS SISTER. I don't think so, I think there's more
significance in the monstrous lake of wee.

JOHN. A loch, Loch Ness?

MRS SISTER. I think so. My sister's got a guest
house up there. I'll give you the number.

JOHN. Thanks a lot Mrs Sister. I'm sorry we
deceived you Harry, will you forgive us and
rejoin the quest?

HARRY. Nae bother . . .

JOHN.   Hello, Mrs McSister, I rang you earlier, about
   three single rooms.
MRS MCSISTER.   Are you all together?
JOHN, TONY *and* HARRY.   Yes.
MRS MCSISTER.   What is it? Business, touring or
   have you come up to get a glimpse of Nessie?
JOHN, TONY *and* HARRY.   Come up to get a glimpse
   of Nessie.
MRS MCSISTER.   My brother hires boats out if you're
   interested.
JOHN, TONY *and* HARRY.   Mumble . . . We're
   interested.
MRS MCSISTER.   Fine; guest house bills are to be
   paid cash in advance and there's to be no
   dominoes in the rooms.
HARRY.   That's a bit steep.
MRS MCSISTER.   I'm sorry but we had one guest
   putting them down the toilet.
JOHN.   What do you know about the holy glasses
   Mrs McSister?
MRS MCSISTER.   Is this something to do with the
   Scottish Arthur?
JOHN.   The Scottish Arthur? Who would that be if
   you don't mind me asking?

MRS MCSISTER.   Arthur King of Scots. The king's great vision was said to stem from a strange crown with see-through bits which he always wore half way down his face. For sixty years he ruled with dignity and control like Bob Holness does on *Blockbusters*. Before he died he cast his crown into the waters of Loch Ness . . .

JOHN.   And the lady caught it on her head and turned into a monster . . .

MRS MCSISTER.   No, that's what was put around centuries ago by the Tourist Board; people were suckers for such metamorphosis stories in those days.

TONY.   So how much does your brother charge to go in the boat?

MRS MCSISTER.   Fifty quid a day.

HARRY.   Very reasonable.

MRS MCSISTER.   Each.

Out of doors. Splash of oars.

TONY.   So why do you think Harry's gone home again?

JOHN.   He thinks it's ridiculous.

TONY.   What, the story about Arthur and the

monster?

JOHN. No, not being able to play dominoes in the room.

TONY. Here John, was Arthur before or after William?

JOHN. Sorry?

TONY. Was William the Conqueror later or earlier than Arthur?

JOHN. Later.

TONY. So how come we're looking in the lake: if the glasses subsequently went down to Hastings and then over to France with William?

JOHN. I don't know, Tony. Can you see anything in that cave?

TONY. I can see something moving in that cave! . . . Oh, no, it's just some eighteenth-century smugglers.

JOHN. I think maybe we need to be a little more active in our search for the monster. I'll try a bit of invocation: Nessie, Nessie can we see you, please say yessie. Anything?

TONY. Nothing.

JOHN. Hold on, I've got another one: Our monster which art in Ness, are you shaped like a letter 's'?

TONY. The waters are parting . . . No, it's just a couple of German U-boats. Hold on there's

another wavering of the tide over by that cave.
Goodness grey-ships! look John, it's worked.
She's here. But where are the glasses?

JOHN.   Oi Nessie where's your glasses?

NESSIE.   I'm sorry but it was too difficult to keep
them on for all those years and all those depths.
I've gone for contact lenses.

JOHN.   But what about the glasses?

NESSIE.   I ate them.

JOHN.   Why?

NESSIE.   Boredom.

TONY.   Did they come out the other end?

NESSIE.   I've been constipated for two thousand
years.

JOHN.   We'll have to kill you and slice you open
then.

NESSIE.   Too messy.

TONY.   Nessie's right.

JOHN.   We've failed.

TONY.   But think of what we've achieved!
Glastonbury, France, Arthurian legends.
Eighteenth-century smugglers, U-boats and now
the Loch Ness Monster.

JOHN.   It's not enough.

TONY.   What more do you want?

JOHN.   Some crisps.

NESSIE.   Here's some. I retrieved them from some

panicking picnickers.

JOHN.   What flavour are they?

NESSIE.   Glasses flavour.

TONY.   Glasses haven't got any flavour.

NESSIE.   And nor have these crisps . . .

HARRY.   Hi, boys, so how did you get on up there?

TONY.   Quite well, but we didn't find the glasses.

JOHN.   A fruitless caper.

HARRY.   Have you seen the paper? They've
    discovered a pile of Loch Ness Monster
    droppings.

JOHN.   Did they describe them in any detail?

HARRY.   They've gone to be examined in a local
    laboratory.

JOHN.   Come on lads. (*Swinging and bringing the
    singing.*)
    We seek the holy glasses
    we seek through thin and thick
    we want to find those glasses
    we think they'll be fantastic.

JOHN.   We're in the lab, fab.

TONY.   Good work with that jemmy, Harry.

HARRY.   Don't shine the torch on the windows!

JOHN.   Can you see anything? Can you smell anything?

TONY.   What's that there?

HARRY.   It's just a pile of old muck.

JOHN.   You've found it! That must have took some shifting.

TONY.   It'll take some sifting as well.

JOHN.   Harry?

TONY.   Hold on. What's that glistening in the torchlight over there . . . on the table? It's a pair of glasses . . . There's a label.

JOHN.   What does it sable?

TONY.   'Found in the mound, and bound for further investigation.'

JOHN.   It's them!

HARRY.   OK. Let's get out of here.

TONY.   Let me have a little try first.

JOHN.   What are they like Tony? Tony what's happened to the torch? What's happened to Tony?!

HARRY.   I think he's gone John.

JOHN.   Tony! Tony!?

HARRY.   Here you are John, two teas, weak as you
    please these, just like you like them. Any news
    from Tony?

JOHN.   I've had a couple of postcards. Look: I think
    he must have sent this one first.

HARRY.   Where's it from?

JOHN.   It's from the ancient Holy Land.

HARRY.   Where?

JOHN.   I know it's crazy, the postmarks are nearly
    two thousand years old.

HARRY.   What does he say?

JOHN.   I'll read the writing.

'So much has happened since I put those glasses
on. I suddenly found myself in a cold cave. For
some reason I thought it was the one where we
saw the smugglers, then I saw this big stone in
the entrance. Luckily I was able to roll it out of
the way. Luckily I had the torch as well. Anyway
when I got outside there were a couple of Roman
soldiers having a kip. Difficult to believe, I
know. Anyway, it's daylight and I follow the
road away from the cave to a small town that
looks rather biblical. By now I've guessed what's
going on. So these eleven blokes come running
out to meet me and I say, "I thought there were
twelve of you." "Judas couldn't make it Lord,"
says one of them. "I don't believe it's him," says

another. "All right Tom," I say, "I know you'd like to feel my wounds but I'm afraid they've healed. Sorry if it's a bit of a disappointment for you!" "Sorry Lord," he says. "No problem," I say, "just tell me how I get back to the twentieth century." Anyway John, I'll keep you up to date on my progress; the post's a bit slow round here as you'll realise if you ever manage to get this. Say hello to Harry, love, Tony.'

HARRY.   It's amazing how much he can fit on one postcard. Nice of him to remember me, isn't it?

JOHN.   Mm. The other one's a different story though. 'Brethren, I send this letter to you as I want to give you hope. I have walked among the people who are sliding on the slope. I have visited the Marys who found it hard to cope and to him called Pontius Pilate I have sent a bar of soap. See you in Paradise.' He hasn't even signed it.

HARRY.   He's obviously not himself.

JOHN.   The only bit of Tony in there is the little joke about Pontius Pilate.

HARRY.   Was that a joke?

JOHN.   Imagine being placed in the context of another time and place; the only way to adapt

and stay sane is to become part of it. The glasses
are turning Tony into the teacher from the tomb.

HARRY.   Why don't you write back and remind him
of his roots?

JOHN.   I don't know his address . . . Sorry Harry, it's
Burry again . . . Hi, Mrs Sister how are you? . . .
Sorry? . . . No!

HARRY.   What's she saying?

JOHN.   The dog says there's a sacred spare pair . . .
OK Mrs Sist. I get the gist, thanks, bye! . . .
They're on your mantelpiece, Harry. Those
glasses we gave you have become the sacred
spare pair by a miracle. Don't tarry, I need those
glasses Harry.

HARRY.   You're taking my present back now are
you; now that you know it might be valuable?

JOHN.   I want to borrow the present to take me into
the past; so I can help Tony and hopefully get
him back here.

HARRY.   OK. Coming right up . . . one spare pair of
holy glasses . . .

JOHN.   Thanks Harry . . . I'm being pulled into
another dimension . . . *Au revoir*.

HARRY.   You haven't paid . . .

TONY.   Ah, Judas. You're back.

JOHN.   Judas!? I'm John and you're Tony and your glasses are filthy.

TONY.   Let us wipe.

JOHN.   Harry, thank the Lord we're back. It was like rubbing the magic lamp. As soon as we wiped our glasses. Shazam.

TONY.   Brethren.

HARRY.   I think he needs a cuppa to calm him down.

JOHN.   These teas are a bit cold Harry.

HARRY.   You've been gone a long time. I think if Tony takes off the glasses it'll be easier for him to reacclimatise.

JOHN.   Tony, give me the glasses.

TONY.   Stand back, get behind me.

JOHN.   Tony . . .

HARRY.   Give him the glasses, go on, you don't want to start getting tied to your possessions.

TONY.   Take them all of you and do not eat of them . . .

JOHN.   Phew. Are you all right Tony?

TONY.   Yeah, just slightly confused, two teas please, Harry. And a couple for yourself.

JOHN.

> We found the holy glasses
> and went around the bend
> of the arms of the holy glasses
> to reach as far as they extend.
> Armends.

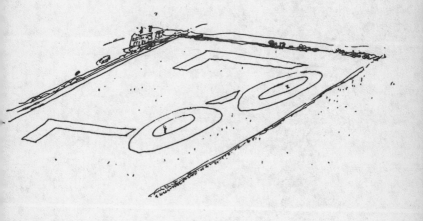

'SO WHO IS THE FATHER, JOSEPH?'

SO WHO IS THE FATHER, JOSEPH

Pop and me

My dad had come along to watch me
the day I came last in the cub scout sack race;
the day my glasses fell off on to the running track
and somebody behind me
deliberately hopped on top of them
and damaged them really badly.
I was that
struggling runt at the back
laughed at by everyone,
everyone, except my dad.
And not because he had
a beating in mind
but because he felt for me.
And when he came to find me
and I was melting with tears
he said 'You're the one
they'll remember in the years to come, son,
you were very funny.'
And he took me to the shop
and ordered me some pop
and we halved the humiliation
when he didn't have the money.

A crisis across the street

They were showing no respect for their elders
I'd have said.
'Come on you filthy old tramp, put your fists up,'
taunted one of a circle of youths
as another punched bunched knuckles
into the back of the unbarbered head.
Sprightly as he could, the man whipped round
to defend himself but span
too far and ended up facing the front again.
It was painfully pathetic
and although the school playground
was the last place I'd been in a fight
I thought I might be able to help him beat these odds
        and sods
but maybe I was being over-ambitious
and maybe they were only mucking about
and he was their dad.

Sandal man

In the heat
on an Indian street,
seeing me hobbling along
in footwear gone wrong
the sandal man eagerly beckons me to his pavement
   pitch.
He begins to stitch the shoes from my feet.
He knows how to wheedle a needle, this man
and I let him continue with his work
even though I know that for all his mending
and rubbing with enriching lacquer
these are sandals knackered beyond repair;
their life span cannot be increased.
I feel like a bald man enjoying the mere motions of a
   haircut;
my sandals are like Randall and Hopkirk:
one of them's deceased.

Mahootman

Carrying out his tasks
above the tusks
our mahoot was almost mute
but it is not his job
to jabber.
His fundamental duty
is to be mahooty.
The mahoot chooses the route
with his toes behind each flapping ear
to tickle the instructions.
His large charge steps steadily through the forest trees
easily squashing down the most vicious of prickles.
Everything is going along happily
until apparently she does something wrong
and the mahoot thwacks her with his stick.
In spite of the thickness of her hide
it ruins my ride
and when I'm back inside the hotel
I tell the man sitting at the tourist desk
how it gave me a shock
and he tells me how a passenger elephant
recently ran amok
and they had to shoot
the mahoot.

The dog and the Hogmanay hotel

It was a hotel up in Scotland
with an English maitre d'
and some not so Scottish customs
it was pointed out to me:
like the haggis-hurling contest
on a wet and windy morn,
every guest was gathered
out of interest on the lawn.
There was little doggie Hamish
who was barking long and loud,
excited at the prospect
of the haggis-hurling crowd;
the maitre d' wore reindeer horns
to chirpy things along
and explained the haggis hurling
to the members of the throng.
'First you choose your haggis
from the ones here in the heap,
then you put the kilt on
but it isn't yours to keep.
You stay within the hurling square
to validate your throw
and swing your haggis discus-like
remembering to let go.'

The people hurled their haggises
and haggis number three
was slightly misdirected
and it hit the maitre d'.
But it wasn't done on purpose
so it didn't make him mad,
he took it in good part he did,
the best part that he had;
he laughed both hail and heartily
and so did all the throng
and Hamish kept on barking
kept on barking loud and long.
The contest was completed
when the whisky had been won
and the winner said that hurling Hamish
would have been more fun.

Christmas past and presents

My brother-in-law's boy
joyfully rips into his motley Christmas pile.
'Gently,'
says my brother-in-law aggressively,
as he absent-mindedly
takes the wrappers off something of his own.
It is the big bird-table from me.
'Mm' he intones appreciatively
'some firewood.'
Smilingly, I lift my gift from him
out of its plastic carrier
and discover a lemonade-making kit
very, very similar to the one I got him last year.

A shilling for my thoughts

I was a lone home-bound passenger
on a long seat on the Underground.
On the space adjacent to me
a five-pence coin was sat.
I did not particularly
want to pick it up to join
my own supply of loose money
but I thought that leaving it there
might leave the next passenger in an embarrassing
    situation:
pocketing it would look cheap
but sitting on it would look stupid,
as would alerting the guard to the loss of such a
    trivial sum.
Thinking it unlikely somebody would come
who was five pence short of their fare
and therefore glad beyond embarrassment,
I placed the coin in my own pocket
as a small contribution to the social good.

Spick and span

My mum was cleaning mad.
Every day was washing day.
Thursday was the brass.
The candlesticks in particular.
She would apply the polish
with such sustained force
that in due course
it seemed she must abolish
their existence.
Or at least bring to pass
the appearance of a genie.
Those candlesticks now stand in my living room
charged with her years of clean living energy
and caked in years of my candle wax.
She would throw a tantrum if she could see them,
or at least find it hard to relax.
My dad was similarly mad about tidying
and both carried out their obsessions to the letter
using so much time which could have been spent so
    much better.
They weren't as grown up as I thought they were.
For which I love them more.

Love poems

Life's
Old
Vast
Emotion

Lips
Of
Venus
Expectant

Lots
Of
Valentine's
Envelopes

Luton
Oh
Veritable
Enigma

Before you ridicule

Remember,
somebody on a railway platform
who seems to be train spotting
may actually be writing poetry.

Poetry strike

Nobody will play
with words
and it will be bad for the economy
of language.

Love cuts

Love cuts
love juts out
and you walk right into it.

Love cuts
love comes and goes
love's a rose
first you smell the flower
then the thorn gets up your nostril
love gives you the chocolates
and then love gives you the chop
it doesn't like to linger.

Love cuts
love shuts up shop
and shuts it on your finger
love cuts
what isn't very nice is
love leaves you in slices.

Love cuts
love's very sharp
a harpoon through an easy chair
a comb of honey in your hair

just wait until the bees come home
and find you just relaxing there.

Love cuts
love's claws
evacuate that heart of yours
and leave it on the sleeve it wipes
its nose on.

Love cuts, love guts the fish
of what you wish for
and leaves it in the airing cupboard.

Love cuts
love huts fall down
as all the walls get falser.

Love cuts
love struts around on stilts of balsa wood
love cuts love gives you a sweeping bow
then ploughs a furrow deep above your eyebrow
love cuts
love curtseys
then nuts you
where it really hurtseys.

Me, Pat and my pet

I first met Pat in Harry's Caff. We got into a chat and she wondered if I would like to come to her flat to sit for her oil-painting portraiture purposes. The following Tuesday I made my way up into the attic where I sat, as she painted and explained her

preoccupation with the early Cubists and her particular obsession with the work of Georges Braque. She had a cubular papier mâché globe which hung from her ceiling, which I described as my favourite exhibit. She laughed and said that it was really just a bit of fun; I said that there was room for fun in art and she agreed. She also explained her frustrated efforts to get shown in a gallery. I said I too had once tried to get a gallery owner interested in my little sketches and he had laughed at them; but not in a nice way. This was to be a trait she would later deplore: the way I would immediately follow any complaint of hers with a similar one of my own, instead of showing her some sympathy. Pat and I were to strike up a considerable relation, something other than a combination of mere sitter and setter in oils. There was something more between us than a piece of canvas; something considerably more. At the end of my second visit, when she looked at the painting and said it was finished, I think we both knew that it was only just beginning. She suggested we spend a weekend away together. We decided upon Grange-over-Sands.

'We can go all the way by train,' I enthused.

'Let's go by coach,' she countered, 'you can snuggle up better in coach seats. It's like being a kid in a den.'

'I do prefer the train,' I persisted.

'Let's go by both,' she bargained.

The resultant compromise was a coach from London to Preston and Preston to Grange by rail. From London to Preston is in the region of two hundred miles and from Preston to Grange around twenty. Years later I would use this instance and these figures as an early example of the degree of compromise of which she was capable. But as I say, that was later on. Now I was just happy to be transported with her in any way the world chose and I eagerly looked forward to our rendezvous at Victoria Coach Station.

On the day, she arrived with a big smile and a little present. I cast aside the wrapping to discover a pocket-sized sketchpad with a charcoal pencil pushed inside the ring-binding. She showed me the same which she had bought for herself but without any wrapping. Previously I had used a 2B pencil. Once a 2B line has been made that's it more or less, but with a charcoal pencil you can rub your line and get a really hot thumb. The resultant smudginess was particularly appropriate for creating the image of smoke coming from the image of a steam train. I drew a few of these dream machines and only once thought what a shame it was that we were actually on a coach.

At the hotel, as well as enjoying the traditional bedroom intimacies and the hotnesses of parts apart from the thumb, much time was spent at our sketchpads, and on the occasions when our subject matter was the same, I actually became quite competitive. But in a loving kind of way. Because the whole time was charmed and charming. At times we were so close it was a little alarming. And we went out into the winter and created a snow dog from the heaven-sent raw material, and I gave him my charcoal pencil as a long thin black eye.

> *Up in Grange-over-Sands*
> *we had love on our hands*
> *and a dog made of snow*
> *and we called him Snowy*
> *and he was so happy*
> *although he had no Chappie.*

That little poem of six weeks into our relationship was called 'We made something beautiful' and it makes contrasting reading to another piece of six years into the relationship entitled 'You make me sick'.

> *You walked into the room*
> *you were in such a mood*
> *and all I did was ask you where my pumps*
> *were.*
> *The fuss that you made*
> *you said I needed a nursemaid*
> *and you threw me my pumps*

and you hit me just above the eye
what a way to treat a guy
you hit me in the head
and you made it all red
I nearly had the tread on my head
it wasn't like having a Med-
iterranean holiday
it started raining
raining training shoes
you threw me my pumps
and you gave me the black and blues
you gave me pain in my heart
and you gave me pain in
the part of me that's got my brain in
and the lace whipped across my face
it could have gashed me
it really lashed me
it's lucky I was wearing my glasses that's all I can
        say
you threw me my pumps
and you gave me lumps.

This piece had the alternative title of 'Fling at Pat's flat'. It was shortly after I had written this that Pat decided to mount an exhibition in her attic instead of awaiting the favourable whim of a gallery owner. And there was someone amongst the invitees whom I recognised from outside my acquaintance with Pat. As soon as he came into the room I placed him, even though it was a couple of decades since I had last encountered him. It was Wojtek. Wojtek, who had stolen my sweetheart of childhood and left me bitter far beyond my years. Wojtek, who had given me the pain by snogging with Jane; he was here again. After they had all gone I asked Pat, 'What were you chatting to Wojtek about then?'

'Oh, you know Wojtek, John? Where from?'

'Just around. What were you saying to him?'

'I was talking to him about the pictures.'

'And what did you write in your diary.'

'He's coming to sit for me.'

'Why's that then?'

'He's got a good bone-structure.'

'No he hasn't.'

'Why, what's wrong with it?'

'It's intact.'

Rather than continuing in this unpleasant manner I thought I'd better get out of the situation. Transform the jealousy I was feeling into something else.

'I'm not happy about it, but I'm not happy about the relationship generally am I, Pat? I think I'm going to go away for the weekend. We need a break.'

I decided to go back to Grange-over-Sands. Sometimes I'm a little lacking in imagination. I took

the train the whole way this time and went back to
the hotel where Snowy was created. It was as I
thought, he was gone, but fortunately I was able to
put myself into the present and seek out my
salvation; I befriended a seventy-six-year-old called
Mrs Phelps who was also a guest in the nest of the
hotel.

On the Sunday evening which was to be our last
together my companion suggested we provide
ourselves with some imaginary sketching
entertainment. She began to make sweeping drawing
movements with an imaginary pencil. When she had
finished she showed me her non-existent page. 'Very
nice,' I adjudged, 'very nice indeed.'

'It's rubbish,' she answered. 'Let's see yours.'

'Here you are.'

'Is that me?'

'Mm.'

'I thought so, very nice.'

I didn't think my effort was that good myself and
so I gave it to her as a present. She then said she had
something for me too and handed me a photograph
of herself, naked. 'That's me when I was twenty-six,'
she said, and there was something boundlessly
appealing about this unreachable beauty whose
source was so close at hand.

At the end of the evening at eight o'clock she bade

me good night and suggested we exchange phone numbers. This I happily agreed to do, although I didn't give her my real one as it was all getting a bit weird.

However, my miserableness had been shifted and arriving back home in London I rang Pat and made my way over to her flat, only to have my newfound enthusiasm dramatically flattened when she told me that she had gone to an art exhibition the previous afternoon with Wojtek.

'If you want to see Boris then you don't see me,' I said trying to demean his existence by giving him the wrong name.

'Don't be stupid John.'

'Stupid? Stupid?? I'll show you what stupid is,' I said rolling about on the floor very stupidly. I was desperate for something to give me the upper hand and had a sudden inspiration. 'Well I spent my time with someone else as well while I was away and I had a fantastic time. Look at this picture she gave me of herself without any clothes on!' Unfortunately Pat could see that it wasn't what I was trying to make out because Mrs Phelps was still holding her ration book. I burst out of the room but not before wishing Pat a happy new relationship in a horrible way, tearing up my photo and sprinkling it over her, saying 'Have some confetti'.

I received a letter from her a couple of days later. It said something along the lines of 'Can't you allow me to get the things I can't get from you from other people? Can't you realise that it means I have more to give you? Can't you? Please?'

I immediately drafted a reply which said: 'NO!'

I wrote it on a sheet of brown paper with a black pastel oil stick. Then I underlined it to make sure she didn't think it said 'ON'. I didn't want her to think I was saying the relationship was on. At the foot of the page I wrote no reply required. I didn't hear from her for nearly two years which was substantially longer than I'd had in mind. I was chopping up an onion when she rang me and she was in tears.

'I need to speak to you.'

'Well I have no desire to speak to you' I said, even though I did. And then I softened and said 'All right, do you want to come round for some food?' And so she came round and I gave her half the onion. And she told me how Wojtek had just got an art exhibition in a gallery and he'd ripped off all her ideas, even the cubular globe, and all the publicity said how he was keeping the spirit of Georges Braque alive and she kept crying and I told her to try and enjoy her meal, humble as it was, and then we went into the living room and I switched on the gas fire and when I lit it the flame didn't go whoof like it sometimes does and

I was glad because it was more calm and she sat on the settee behind me and I had the warmth of the fire in front of me and the warmth of her presence behind. It was a miracle her returning, even though she had opened the door and come through it in an ordinary way, it was a miracle. She had returned and I never thought she could and we never spoke for ages, we just sat, me and Pat and then she said, 'I've missed you so much, I'm so fond of you, you're beautiful.' And I turned around and she was talking to the dog.

On the pavement

Sauntering along alone I hear other busier footsteps
    behind me.
Not feeling threatened but awkward
I wonder, should I slow down my walking
and let them get by as soon as possible
or shall I imperceptibly quicken to a higher gear
before they are near enough to notice?
Ah, it's OK, it sounds like they've just fallen over.